GOOGLER

INSIDE GOOGLE HIRINGS: NAVIGATING CHALLENGES AND HELPING OTHERS SUCCEED

PRASHANT PANDEY

For my parents, who always encouraged me to dream big and supported me in every step of my journey. For my mentors and colleagues, who challenged me to be my best self and helped me grow both personally and professionally. And for all the aspiring engineers and job seekers out there, who inspire me to keep learning and giving back. This book is dedicated to you

Contents

Contents

Contents

Foreword

In today's fast-paced and constantly evolving tech industry, landing a job at a company like Google can seem like an insurmountable challenge. Yet, for Prashant Pandey, it was not only possible but also something he helped many others achieve. In this book, Prashant offers a firsthand account of his experiences as a Machine Learning Engineer at Google, and shares his insights on what it takes to succeed in the tech industry.

Prashant's story is an inspiring one, as he not only accomplished his own goals, but also went above and beyond to help others reach their own dreams of working at Google. In these pages, you will find a wealth of practical advice on how to navigate the complex world of tech recruitment, as well as the personal stories of those who have succeeded in the field.

This book is a must-read for anyone who is interested in working in the tech industry, or for those who are currently on the job hunt. Prashant's dedication to helping others succeed, along with his wealth of knowledge and experience, make this book an invaluable resource for anyone looking to build a successful career in the tech industry.

Preface

As a Machine Learning Engineer at Google, I had the opportunity to work with some of the brightest minds in the industry, and to help many others realize their own dreams of working at one of the world's most elite companies. Through my experience, I have learned that the process of getting hired in the tech industry can be a daunting and challenging journey, filled with its own set of unique obstacles and opportunities.

In this book, I aim to provide an honest and practical guide to help those who are interested in pursuing a career in tech, or those who are currently navigating the job market. I share my experiences working at Google and helping others succeed in the industry, as well as insights on the hiring process, interview techniques, and tips for career advancement.

My hope is that this book will not only serve as a valuable resource for those seeking employment in the tech industry, but also as a source of inspiration for anyone who is working hard to achieve their goals. I believe that with the right mindset, preparation, and determination, anyone can achieve success in the tech industry.

Thank you for joining me on this journey, and I hope that the insights and advice presented in this book will help you achieve your own dreams of working in the exciting and dynamic world of tech.

Prashant Pandey

Acknowledgements

Writing this book has been a labor of love, and it would not have been possible without the support and encouragement of many people.

Firstly, I would like to express my gratitude to my family, who have been my constant source of inspiration and support throughout my life. Their unwavering love and encouragement have given me the strength to pursue my dreams and never give up.

I would like to extend my heartfelt thanks to my mentors and colleagues at Google, who have taught me so much and challenged me to be my best self. Their guidance, advice, and friendship have been invaluable in shaping my career and shaping me as a person.

I am also grateful to the many job seekers whom I have helped over the years. Their stories have inspired me, and their feedback and questions have helped shape the content of this book. I am honored to have been a part of their journey to success.

Finally, I would like to thank my readers, who have taken the time to read this book and learn from my experiences. I hope that this book has been of help to you and that it has provided valuable insights into the exciting and dynamic world of tech.

Thank you all for your support, encouragement, and inspiration.

Prashant Pandey

Prologue

I still remember the day I received the offer letter from Google. It was a moment of pure excitement and joy, and I felt like all my hard work and persistence had finally paid off. As a Machine Learning Engineer, I had the opportunity to work on cutting-edge projects and collaborate with some of the brightest minds in the industry. It was a dream come true.

However, as I soon found out, working at Google was not without its challenges. The fast-paced and ever-changing nature of the tech industry required me to constantly stay on top of my game, adapt to new technologies, and be open to new ideas. And as I watched many others struggle to land their dream job, I realized that getting hired at Google was not an easy feat.

Through my experience at Google and my work helping others succeed, I have come to understand the unique challenges and opportunities of working in the tech industry. In this book, I share my personal journey, as well as the lessons I have learned about the hiring process, interview techniques, and career advancement.

My hope is that this book will serve as a guide for those who are seeking employment in the tech industry, or those who are looking to advance their careers. I believe that with the right mindset, preparation, and determination, anyone can achieve success in this exciting and dynamic field.

Thank you for joining me on this journey, and I hope that the insights and advice presented in this book will help you achieve your own goals and aspirations.

Prashant Pandey

CHAPTER ONE

The founding of Google and the first office

The founding of Google marked the beginning of a technological revolution that has changed the world. In the late 1990s, Larry Page and Sergey Brin, two computer science students at Stanford University, developed a new approach to web search and set out to build a search engine that could change the way people find information online.

Page and Brin's initial concept, called BackRub, used a unique algorithm that considered the number and quality of links pointing to a website as an indicator of its relevance and importance. As they continued to refine their algorithm, they began to focus on a concept they called PageRank, which took into account not just the quantity of links but also the relevance of the content on the site.

With their innovative approach to search, Page and Brin began to attract attention and soon realized they had a business opportunity on their hands. In September 1998, they founded Google, a play on the word "googol," a mathematical term for the number represented by the numeral 1 followed by 100 zeros.

Initially, Google was run out of a dorm room at Stanford, with Page and Brin working on computers borrowed from the university. As the company grew, they moved into their first official office, a small space in a nondescript office park in Menlo Park, California.

The office, which was just over 1,000 square feet, was modest by Silicon Valley standards. It was furnished with inexpensive office furniture and had a ping-pong table in the center of the room. Despite its humble beginnings, the office quickly became the hub of Google's early operations.

At the Menlo Park office, Page and Brin assembled a small team of engineers and began to develop the technology that would make Google the most popular search engine in the world. They focused on building a simple, intuitive interface that emphasized speed and accuracy and made it easy for users to find what they were looking for.

As Google's popularity grew, the Menlo Park office became too small, and the company moved to a larger space in Mountain View, California. But the spirit of innovation and collaboration that characterized the early days of Google remained a defining feature of the company's culture.

Today, Google is one of the most valuable companies in the world, with a market capitalization of over $1 trillion. Its search engine handles billions of searches every day, and the company has diversified into a wide range of other businesses, including cloud computing, advertising, and artificial intelligence.

In conclusion, the founding of Google and the opening of its first official office in Menlo Park, California, marked the beginning of a transformative period in the history of the internet. Larry Page and Sergey Brin's innovative approach to search and their focus on user experience helped make Google the most popular search engine in the world and set the stage for the company's continued success.

CHAPTER TWO

The early years of Larry Page and Sergey Brin

Larry Page and Sergey Brin, the co-founders of Google, are two of the most successful entrepreneurs of our time. Their story began in the early 1990s when they were both students at Stanford University.

Page grew up in Michigan and was interested in computers from a young age. He attended the University of Michigan before transferring to Stanford to pursue a graduate degree in computer science. Brin, on the other hand, was born in Russia and came to the United States as a child. He also studied at the University of Maryland before enrolling at Stanford, where he pursued a graduate degree in computer science.

It was at Stanford that Page and Brin first met, in 1995. They were both working on their own individual projects but found themselves collaborating on a search engine called BackRub. BackRub used a unique algorithm to rank web pages based on their popularity, which was a significant departure from the traditional method of using keywords to identify relevant content.

In 1996, Page and Brin decided to formalize their partnership and founded Google, with the mission of organizing the world's information and making it universally accessible and useful. They initially worked out of their dorm rooms, building and refining their search algorithm.

By 1998, Google was gaining traction, and Page and Brin began seeking funding to grow their business. They received $100,000 from Andy Bechtolsheim, co-founder of Sun Microsystems, and soon after secured a total of $1 million in funding.

As Google grew, Page and Brin continued to focus on improving the user experience and expanding the company's offerings. In 2001, they introduced AdWords, a program that allowed businesses to advertise on Google's search results pages. AdWords was a huge success and helped Google become profitable for the first time.

Today, Google is one of the most valuable companies in the world, and Page and Brin are two of the wealthiest people on the planet. They have since stepped down from their day-to-day roles at Google but remain involved as board members and advisors.

In summary, the early years of Larry Page and Sergey Brin were marked by a passion for computer science and a commitment to innovation. They collaborated on a groundbreaking search engine, founded Google, and continued to innovate and grow the company into the global behemoth it is today.

Their initial ideas for search algorithms and web ranking

Larry Page and Sergey Brin, the co-founders of Google, are widely known for their groundbreaking search engine and their innovative approach to ranking web pages. Their early ideas for search algorithms and web ranking played a significant role in the development of Google and the evolution of the internet.

Page and Brin's initial idea for a search engine, BackRub, was a departure from traditional methods of web search, which relied on keywords to identify relevant content. Instead, they developed an algorithm that considered a website's links as a key indicator of its importance.

The idea behind this approach was that websites with more links pointing to them were likely to be more authoritative and relevant. By analyzing the structure of the web, Page and Brin were able to build a search engine that provided more accurate and useful results than other search engines of the time.

As they continued to refine their algorithm, Page and Brin began to focus on a concept called PageRank, which was named after Larry Page. PageRank took into account the quality and quantity of links pointing to a website, as well as the relevance of the content on the site.

PageRank allowed Google to differentiate itself from other search engines and provided a more reliable way to rank websites. Instead of relying on keyword density or other easily manipulated factors, PageRank considered the entire ecosystem of the web to determine the relative importance of a given site.

By the late 1990s, Google had emerged as a dominant force in the search engine market, and its unique approach to web ranking had become a key differentiator. In addition to its sophisticated algorithms, Google also emphasized the importance of user experience and simplicity, which made it more appealing to users than other search engines.

Over time, Google continued to refine its search algorithms and add new features, such as personalized search results and local search. The company's focus on innovation and user experience has helped it maintain its dominance in the search engine market for over two decades.

In summary, Larry Page and Sergey Brin's initial ideas for search algorithms and web ranking were based on a unique approach to analyzing the structure of the web. Their PageRank algorithm, which considered the quality and quantity of links pointing to a website, set Google apart from other search engines and laid the foundation for its continued success. Their focus on innovation and user experience has helped make Google the most popular search engine in the world.

CHAPTER FOUR

Understanding the Google company culture and values

Google is one of the most well-known and respected companies in the world. With its reputation for innovation and excellence, it is no surprise that so many people aspire to work there. But landing a job at Google is no easy feat. The company is selective and rigorous in its hiring process, and it is important to understand its culture and values in order to be a competitive candidate. In this article, we will explore what makes the Google culture unique and what the company values in its employees.

Company Culture

Google's company culture is often described as being focused on creativity, collaboration, and innovation. This is reflected in its work environment, which is designed to foster creativity and collaboration between employees. For example, Google's offices are known for their open and flexible work spaces, which encourage employees to work together and share ideas. The company also places a strong emphasis on work-life balance, with benefits such as flexible hours, unlimited vacation time, and on-site amenities like gyms and cafes.

One of the key aspects of Google's culture is its focus on employee empowerment. The company believes that its employees are its greatest asset, and it provides them with the resources and support they need to succeed. This includes training programs, mentorship opportunities, and access to cutting-edge technology. Google also encourages employees to take risks and to pursue their passions, even if it means pursuing projects that are outside of their normal job responsibilities.

Values

Google's culture is guided by a set of values that are closely aligned with its mission and vision. These values are embodied in the company's policies and practices, and they play a critical role in shaping the work environment and employee experience. The following are some of the key values that drive the Google culture:

Focus on the user: Google's top priority is always the user. The company is committed to creating products and services that are user-friendly and that make a real difference in people's lives.

Innovation: Google is known for its innovative approach to problem-solving, and it encourages employees to think outside the box and to pursue creative solutions.

Collaboration: Google values collaboration and teamwork, and it seeks to create an environment where employees can work together effectively and efficiently.

Objectivity: Google places a high value on data-driven decision-making and objective analysis. The company seeks to make decisions based on the facts, rather than personal opinions or biases.

Openness: Google values transparency and open communication, and it encourages employees to share their ideas and opinions openly and honestly.

Responsibility: Google is committed to doing the right thing and to making a positive impact in the world. The company is guided by a strong sense of ethics and social responsibility.

Focus on growth: Google is focused on continuous learning and growth, and it provides employees with the resources and support they need to develop their skills and grow professionally.

Google is known for its unique company culture and values, which have played a significant role in the company's success. Here are some key points that define the Google culture and values:

Innovation: Google encourages innovation and creativity among its employees. The company provides resources and support to help employees pursue new ideas and initiatives.

Transparency: Google values transparency in all aspects of the company's operations. The company shares information with its employees and the public, and strives to maintain open communication channels.

Collaboration: Google emphasizes the importance of collaboration and teamwork. The company provides a supportive and inclusive work environment that fosters collaboration and encourages diverse perspectives.

Respect: Google values respect for individuals and diversity. The company promotes a culture of inclusivity and strives to create a work environment where everyone feels valued and respected.

Focus on Users: Google prioritizes the needs of its users and strives to create products and services that are useful and relevant to them.

Data-Driven: Google relies on data to make informed decisions and to measure the effectiveness of its products and initiatives.

Agility: Google operates in a fast-paced and constantly changing industry, and the company values agility and adaptability in its employees. The company encourages its employees to be flexible and to embrace change.

Overall, Google's company culture and values prioritize innovation, collaboration, transparency, and respect for individuals and diversity. These values have helped the company attract and retain top talent, and have played a significant role in its success.

Conclusion

Google's company culture and values set it apart from other organizations, and they play a critical role in shaping the employee experience. Understanding these values and aligning with them is critical to being a competitive candidate for a job at Google. By embracing the company's focus on creativity, collaboration, and innovation, and by demonstrating a commitment to the company's values, you can set yourself apart from the competition and increase your chances of landing your dream job at Google.

CHAPTER FIVE

Understanding the Role of the CEO of Google

The CEO of a company plays a critical role in shaping the direction and success of the organization. This is especially true for a company like Google, which is one of the largest and most influential technology companies in the world. The CEO of Google is responsible for overseeing the strategic direction of the company, setting the tone for the company culture, and guiding the organization through both challenges and opportunities. In this article, we will explore the role of the CEO of Google and the key responsibilities that come with this position.

Strategic Leadership

The CEO of Google is responsible for providing strategic leadership to the company. This involves setting the vision for the company, defining the company's mission, and developing a strategy to achieve these goals. The CEO must also be able to articulate this vision to employees, stakeholders, and the public, and to inspire and motivate others to work towards these goals.

One of the key challenges facing the CEO of Google is balancing the company's desire for innovation and growth with the need to maintain profitability and to generate returns for shareholders. The CEO must be able to make difficult decisions, such as choosing which projects to invest in, and when to cut projects that are not performing well.

Culture and Talent Management

The CEO of Google also plays a critical role in shaping the company culture and in managing the company's talent. The CEO must be able to create an environment that fosters creativity, collaboration, and innovation, and that attracts and retains top talent. This involves developing and implementing policies and practices that promote work-life balance, encourage employee engagement and empowerment, and provide opportunities for professional development.

The CEO of Google must also be able to manage and develop the company's talent, providing opportunities for employees to grow and succeed. This includes providing mentorship opportunities, investing in training and development programs, and recognizing and rewarding top performers.

Representing the Company

The CEO of Google is also responsible for representing the company and its interests to a variety of stakeholders. This includes communicating with shareholders, customers, employees, and the public. The CEO must be able to articulate the company's vision, mission, and strategy, and to respond to questions and concerns from stakeholders.

The CEO of Google must also be able to manage the company's reputation, both internally and externally. This involves addressing issues such as privacy and security, and ensuring that the company is seen as a responsible and ethical corporate citizen.

Problem Solving and Decision Making

The CEO of Google must be able to make tough decisions and to solve complex problems. This involves analyzing data, considering multiple perspectives, and making informed decisions that are in the best interest of the company and its stakeholders.

One of the key challenges facing the CEO of Google is navigating the rapidly changing technology landscape. The CEO must be able to identify trends and opportunities, and to make decisions that ensure the company remains competitive and relevant.

Conclusion

The role of the CEO of Google is complex and demanding, but it is also incredibly rewarding. The CEO is responsible for setting the direction and vision for the company, shaping the company culture, and representing the company to a variety of stakeholders. To be successful in this role, the CEO must be a strategic thinker, an effective communicator, and a problem solver. With its focus on innovation and growth, Google is one of the most exciting and dynamic companies in the world, and the CEO has a critical role to play in shaping its future success.

CHAPTER SIX

Preparing for your Google interview: researching the company and practicing common interview questions

Getting an interview with Google is a great accomplishment and a valuable opportunity to showcase your skills and experience. However, preparing for an interview with such a well-known and competitive company can be overwhelming. In this article, we will discuss the key steps you should take to prepare for your Google interview, including researching the company and practicing common interview questions.

Research the Company

The first step in preparing for your Google interview is to research the company. This includes understanding the company's mission, values, and culture, as well as its products, services, and industry. Researching the company will give you a better understanding of what the company is looking for in a candidate and help you tailor your responses to the specific role and company.

There are a variety of resources available for researching Google, including the company's website, annual reports, and news articles. You can also search for online forums, such as LinkedIn and Glassdoor, where current and former employees discuss their experiences working for the company. By talking to people who have worked for Google, you can get a better understanding of the company culture, the types of projects employees work on, and the skills and experience that are valued.

Practice Common Interview Questions

In addition to researching the company, it is also important to practice common interview questions. Google is known for its unique and challenging interview process, which often includes behavioral and technical questions. Behavioral questions are designed to assess your skills and experience, while technical questions test your knowledge of specific programming languages or concepts.

To prepare for these questions, it is important to review your resume and your experience in detail. This will help you identify your strengths and weaknesses and give you a better understanding of what types of questions you are likely to be asked.

Here are some common interview questions that you may encounter during a Google interview:

Can you tell us about a time when you had to solve a complex problem?

Can you explain a technical concept or programming language that you are familiar with?

Can you describe a project you worked on that required collaboration with others?

How do you handle conflict or disagreements in the workplace?

Can you describe a time when you had to adapt to a change in the workplace?

How do you prioritize tasks and manage your time effectively?

Can you describe a project you worked on that required creativity and innovation?

How do you stay up-to-date with industry trends and technology advancements?

Can you tell us about a time when you took the initiative to solve a problem or improve a process?

Can you describe a time when you had to deal with a difficult customer or co-worker?

To practice these questions, you can use a mirror or a friend or family member to help you practice your responses. Make sure you take your time and think through your answers, and try to provide specific examples and details to support your response. This will help you feel more confident and prepared during the interview.

Preparing for a Google interview can be challenging, but with the right preparation, you can increase your chances of success. By researching the company and practicing common interview questions, you can showcase your skills and experience, and demonstrate why you are the right candidate for the role. Good luck!

The interview process at Google India typically involves several stages and can vary depending on the specific role you are applying for. Here is an overview of the typical interview process for Google India:

Resume Screening: The first stage of the interview process is a review of your resume and cover letter. If your qualifications and experience match the requirements of the role, you will be invited to participate in further stages of the interview process.

Phone Screen: The next stage of the interview process is typically a phone screen, where you will speak with a member of the HR team or a recruiter. During this call, you will be asked a series of questions about your background and experience, and you will have the opportunity to ask questions about the role and the company.

Online Tests: Some roles may require you to complete online tests, such as a programming or coding challenge, or a logic and reasoning test. These tests are designed to assess your technical skills and ability to solve problems.

On-Site Interviews: If you pass the initial stages of the interview process, you will be invited to participate in an on-site interview. This typically involves a series of individual and group interviews with members of the hiring team, including managers and team members. During these interviews, you will be asked a combination of behavioral and technical questions, and you may be asked to complete a case study or problem-solving exercise.

Final Review: After the on-site interviews, the hiring team will review the results of your interviews and assessments, and make a final decision about whether to extend an offer.

Throughout the interview process, it is important to be prepared and to demonstrate your skills, experience, and fit with the company culture. You should research the company and the role in advance, and practice answering common interview questions. You should also be prepared to ask thoughtful questions about the role and the company, and to demonstrate your enthusiasm and passion for the role.

The interview process at Google India can be competitive, but with the right preparation and a strong demonstration of your skills and experience, you can increase your chances of success and land the job of your dreams.

Google is one of the world's leading technology companies, and the interview process at Google is known for being rigorous and competitive. If you are preparing for a Google interview in the United States, it is essential to do your research and be well prepared.

In this article, we will provide tips and guidance on how to research the company and prepare for your Google interview, including:

Understanding Google's Mission and Values: One of the key things to research when preparing for a Google interview is the company's mission and values. Google's mission is to organize the world's information and make it universally accessible and useful, and the company's values are focused on creating an open and innovative workplace where everyone feels valued. Understanding these values and how they guide the company's culture can help you demonstrate your fit with the company during the interview process.

Researching the Role and the Team: Another important aspect of preparing for a Google interview is researching the specific role you are applying for and the team you will be joining. You can do this by reviewing the job description, researching the team's mission and goals, and reading about recent projects and initiatives the team has been working on.

Preparing for Behavioral and Technical Questions: Google's interview process typically involves a combination of behavioral and technical questions, and it is important to be prepared for both. Behavioral questions may include questions about your experience, leadership style, and problem-solving skills, while technical questions may focus on your expertise in a specific area, such as coding or data analysis.

Practicing Common Interview Questions: Practicing common interview questions can help you feel more confident and prepared for your interview. Some common interview questions at Google include "What motivates you?" and "Can you describe a time when you had to overcome a difficult challenge at work?" Practicing these questions and others can help you formulate clear and concise answers that demonstrate your skills and experience.

Demonstrating Passion and Enthusiasm: Google is known for its innovative and fast-paced work environment, and demonstrating your passion and enthusiasm for the company and the role is an important part of the interview process. Be sure to come prepared with thoughtful questions about the company and the role, and be ready to discuss your interest in and excitement for the opportunity to join the team.

By following these tips and doing your research, you can increase your chances of success in the Google interview process and make a strong impression on the hiring team. Good luck!

Google is one of the largest technology companies in the world, known for its innovative products and services. The company has a highly sophisticated sales process and hiring process to ensure that they bring in the best talent and provide the best service to their clients.

The Google sales process starts with a deep understanding of the customer's needs and business objectives. Google sales representatives work closely with the customer to understand their unique challenges and goals, and then develop a customized solution that meets those needs. This solution may involve one or more of Google's products or services, including Google Ads, Google Cloud, and Google Workspace.

Once the solution has been developed, the Google sales representative presents it to the customer and works with them to negotiate the terms and conditions of the agreement. This process typically involves several rounds of negotiations and is designed to ensure that both parties are satisfied with the final agreement.

In terms of hiring, Google is known for its rigorous and comprehensive hiring process. The company's focus on hiring the best talent means that the process can be quite demanding, with multiple rounds of interviews, written tests, and assessments.

The first step in the hiring process is submitting an application, which is then reviewed by a team of recruiters. If the application is deemed a good fit, the candidate is invited to complete a phone interview, which is followed by an on-site interview if the candidate is still being considered.

The on-site interview process is where Google really shines. It typically consists of several rounds of interviews with members of the team the candidate would be working with, as well as assessments designed to evaluate the candidate's technical and communication skills. The assessments may include coding exercises, case studies, and presentations, among other things.

Finally, the hiring process ends with an offer being made to the successful candidate. This offer may include a salary, benefits, and stock options, depending on the position and level of experience of the candidate.

In conclusion, Google's sales process and hiring process are designed to ensure that they bring in the best talent and provide the best service to their customers. The company's rigorous and comprehensive approach to hiring and its focus on understanding the customer's needs have helped it establish a reputation as one of the most innovative and successful technology companies in the world.

CHAPTER SEVEN

The different stages of the Google interview process and what to expect at each stage

Google is widely recognized as one of the most innovative and successful tech companies in the world. As such, the interview process is highly competitive and rigorous, designed to identify the best candidates for the company's unique culture and values. In this article, we'll take a closer look at the different stages of the Google interview process and what to expect at each stage.

Stage 1: Resume Screening and Initial Phone Interview

The first stage of the Google interview process begins with a review of your resume and cover letter. The HR team will be looking for relevant experience, education, and skills that match the position you are applying for. If your resume is selected, you'll then be contacted for an initial phone interview, usually conducted by a recruiter. This phone interview is a screening call to determine whether you're a good fit for the role and for Google's culture.

What to Expect: During the initial phone interview, you'll be asked about your experience, skills, and why you're interested in the position. The interviewer will also ask about your availability and salary expectations. This stage is a great opportunity to ask questions about the company and the role you're applying for, so be prepared to ask thoughtful questions.

Tips: To prepare for the initial phone interview, research the company and the role you're applying for, and be ready to explain how your skills and experience make you a good fit. It's also important to be friendly, confident, and professional during the call.

Stage 2: Technical Interview

If you successfully complete the initial phone interview, the next step is a technical interview. This stage of the interview process is designed to evaluate your technical skills, knowledge, and problem-solving abilities. The technical interview may be conducted in person or via video call, and you may be asked to complete a coding challenge or take a test.

What to Expect: During the technical interview, you'll be asked to solve complex problems and explain your thought process. You may also be asked to write code or debug code samples. You'll also be asked questions about your experience with specific technologies and programming languages. The interviewer may also ask you to design a system or discuss trade-offs in design choices.

Tips: To prepare for the technical interview, brush up on your coding skills and become familiar with the technologies and programming languages relevant to the position you're applying for. It's also a good idea to practice solving complex problems and explaining your thought process.

Stage 3: Onsite Interviews

If you pass the technical interview, the next step is an onsite interview. This stage is designed to evaluate your technical skills and problem-solving abilities in a more comprehensive and interactive manner. You'll also have the opportunity to meet with potential team members and see the office and work environment.

What to Expect: The onsite interview is typically a full-day event, and you may have several interviews with different team members, including managers, senior engineers, and other stakeholders. The interviews may include a mix of technical questions, problem-solving exercises, and behavioral questions. You'll also have the opportunity to meet with potential team members and see the office and work environment.

Tips: To prepare for the onsite interview, research the company, the role you're applying for, and the team you'll be working with. You should also practice your technical skills and problem-solving abilities, and be prepared to answer behavioral questions and talk about your experience and qualifications. It's also important to dress professionally and be punctual for your interviews.

Stage 4: Offer and Negotiations

If you successfully complete the onsite interview, the final step

Few Interview Questions

Can you tell us about your experience in the technology industry?

What are your strengths and weaknesses as a software engineer?

Can you give an example of a difficult problem you solved and how you approached it?

Can you explain how you would optimize a slow-running algorithm?

Can you describe a project you worked on that showcases your coding skills?

How do you stay current with the latest developments in technology?

Can you discuss your experience with agile methodologies?

Can you tell us about a time when you had to work with a team to complete a project?

Can you walk us through your process for debugging a complex issue?

Can you explain the concept of OOP and give an example of how you have used it in your projects?

Can you discuss your experience with cloud computing and the different cloud providers you have worked with?

Can you describe a time when you had to deal with conflicting priorities and how you handled it?

How do you handle difficult technical challenges and what steps do you take to overcome them?

Can you describe a time when you had to work with a difficult team member and how you handled the situation?

Can you explain the concept of data structures and how you have used them in your projects?

Can you discuss your experience with SQL and NoSQL databases?

Can you describe a project you worked on that involved data analysis and how you approached it?

How do you handle new projects or technologies that you are not familiar with?

Can you discuss your experience with software testing and quality assurance?

Can you give an example of a time when you had to balance technical requirements with business goals?

Can you explain how you handle project requirements that are constantly changing?

Can you discuss your experience with version control systems and the different tools you have used?

Can you explain how you handle conflict resolution and negotiate compromises in a team environment?

Can you discuss your experience with microservices and how you have used them in your projects?

Can you describe a time when you had to make a tough technical decision and how you approached it?

Can you discuss your experience with containerization and the different tools you have used?

Can you give an example of a time when you had to work under tight deadlines and how you managed it?

Can you explain the concept of scalability and how you have implemented it in your projects?

Can you discuss your experience with security and how you have implemented security measures in your projects?

Can you describe a time when you had to lead a project from start to finish?

Can you explain the concept of continuous integration and continuous delivery and how you have used them in your projects?

Can you discuss your experience with DevOps and the different tools you have used?

Can you describe a time when you had to debug a production issue and how you approached it?

Can you explain the concept of service-oriented architecture and how you have used it in your projects?

Can you discuss your experience with mobile development and the different platforms you have worked with?

Can you describe a time when you had to implement a new feature with limited resources and how you approached it?

Can you discuss your experience with front-end development and the different tools and frameworks you have used?

Can you explain the concept of test-driven development and how you have used it in your projects?

Can you discuss your experience with code

In conclusion, the Google interview process can be a long and challenging journey, but with the right preparation and mindset, it is definitely worth the effort. The process is designed to assess not only your technical skills but also your ability to work collaboratively, think creatively, and adapt to new challenges.

How to demonstrate your skills, knowledge, and experience during the interview

The Google interview process is renowned for being challenging, rigorous and comprehensive. Many aspiring candidates who apply for a position at the company want to demonstrate their skills, knowledge and experience to the best of their ability during the interview process. This is because a Google interview is not just an opportunity to land a job, but also a chance to be a part of one of the world's most innovative and respected technology companies.

The following are some tips and strategies for demonstrating your skills, knowledge, and experience during the Google interview:

Research the company and the role you are applying for: Before you step into the interview room, it is important to have a good understanding of the company and the role you are applying for. Research the company's mission, values, and culture, as well as the specific responsibilities and requirements of the role. This will enable you to tailor your responses to the interviewer's questions and show that you are a good fit for the company.

Brush up on your technical skills: Google is known for its technical aptitude, so it is important to be confident in your technical skills. Brush up on your coding skills, algorithms, data structures, and other areas relevant to your role. Make sure that you have a deep understanding of the technologies you have used in the past and be prepared to explain your experience and how you used them to solve problems.

Prepare for behavioral questions: In addition to technical questions, Google interviewers also ask behavioral questions. These questions are designed to assess your ability to handle challenges, work in a team, and think critically. Prepare for these questions by thinking about situations you have faced in the past and how you dealt with them. Be ready to provide specific examples and explain your thought process.

Show your passion for technology: Google values passion for technology and innovation. During the interview, show your excitement and enthusiasm for technology and explain why you are passionate about it. Share any projects or initiatives you have worked on in the past that demonstrate your passion for technology.

Be confident and honest: Confidence and honesty are important qualities that Google values. Be confident in your answers and don't be afraid to admit if you don't know something. Instead, show your willingness to learn and be transparent about your limitations. Honesty is always the best policy, and Google interviewers appreciate candidates who are honest about their skills and experiences.

Demonstrate your problem-solving skills: Google interviewers are looking for candidates who can think critically and solve complex problems. During the interview, show your problem-solving skills by explaining how you approached and solved a challenging problem in the past. Explain your thought process and the steps you took to arrive at a solution.

Show your teamwork skills: Google values collaboration and teamwork, so it's important to demonstrate your ability to work well with others. During the interview, share examples of times when you worked on a team project and explain your role and contribution to the project's success.

Be prepared to discuss your experiences and projects: Google interviewers often ask candidates to discuss their past experiences and projects in detail. Be prepared to talk about your experience, the technologies you used, and the results you achieved. Be sure to highlight your accomplishments and show how you made an impact in your previous role.

Ask relevant and thoughtful questions: At the end of the interview, you will be given the opportunity to ask questions. Take advantage of this opportunity to demonstrate your interest in the company and the role. Ask relevant and thoughtful questions that show your understanding of the company and the role.

Google is one of the most sought-after employers in the technology industry, known for its challenging and innovative work environment. The company's hiring process is rigorous and competitive, with a focus on identifying candidates who possess the necessary skills, experience, and cultural fit. In this article, we will explore how to demonstrate your skills during a Google interview and increase your chances of securing a role at the company.

Research the Company and the Role:

Before you even begin preparing for your Google interview, it's important to understand the company's values, mission, and culture. Research the role you're applying for and understand the required skills and experience for the position. Familiarize yourself with the company's products, services, and recent news. This research will not only help you to understand the company better but also give you a better understanding of what the interviewer is looking for.

Showcase Your Technical Skills:

Google is a technology company, and it's important to demonstrate your technical skills in order to secure a role. Prepare for technical questions that might be asked in the interview and be prepared to walk the interviewer through your problem-solving process. Be prepared to talk about your experience with programming languages, data structures, algorithms, and software development. Make sure you understand the basics of computer science and have a good understanding of how things work under the hood.

Communicate Your Passion for Technology:

Google values individuals who are passionate about technology and are always looking for new and innovative ways to improve processes. Show your enthusiasm for the industry and the role you're applying for by speaking about your favorite technology-related topics, including new developments and trends in the field. You can also demonstrate your passion by participating in hackathons, coding challenges, or attending technology conferences and events.

Be Prepared to Discuss Projects:

Google is interested in seeing the projects you've worked on and the skills you've developed through those projects. Be prepared to discuss the projects you've worked on and how they demonstrate your technical skills and experience. Provide examples of how you solved problems and overcame challenges. Explain the impact your projects have had and what you learned from the experience.

Show Your Problem-Solving Skills:

Google is a company that values problem-solving skills. The interviewer may ask you to solve a problem on the spot or discuss how you would solve a hypothetical problem. Be prepared to talk about your problem-solving process, including the steps you would take to identify the problem, gather information, and develop a solution. Emphasize your ability to think critically and your experience with finding creative solutions to complex problems.

Highlight Your Leadership Experience:

Google is a company that values leadership skills, so it's important to showcase any leadership experience you have. This can include leading a team on a project, managing a group of people, or taking initiative to solve a problem. Be prepared to talk about your leadership style and how you approach decision-making. Discuss the challenges you faced and how you overcame them. Highlight your ability to motivate others and how you've helped your team achieve their goals.

Practice Behavioral Interviewing Techniques:

Google often uses behavioral interviewing techniques to assess a candidate's fit for the role. In a behavioral interview, the interviewer will ask you to describe specific situations and how you handled them. Be prepared to talk about your previous work experiences and how you handled challenging situations. Show your ability to work well under pressure and how you respond to challenges. Emphasize your ability to work well with others and your experience with collaborating on projects.

In conclusion, demonstrating your skills during a Google interview requires a combination of technical knowledge, passion for technology, problem-solving skills, leadership experience, and the ability to adapt to change. By preparing for the interview, researching the company and the role, and showcasing your experience, you can increase your chances of securing a role at Google. Remember to be confident and be yourself, as Google values individuals who are authentic and bring their unique strengths to the table. Good luck in your interview and take the time to reflect on your experience and what you learned, as this will help you to continue to grow and develop your skills.

CHAPTER NINE

Tips for communicating effectively and showcasing your personality during the interview

In addition to demonstrating your technical skills and experience, it's also important to effectively communicate during a Google interview and showcase your personality. Google values individuals who are able to work well with others, have strong communication skills, and bring a unique perspective to the table. In this article, we will explore tips for effectively communicating and showcasing your personality during a Google interview.

Be Confident and Authentic:

Google values individuals who are authentic and bring their unique strengths to the table. It's important to be confident and be yourself during the interview, as the interviewer is looking to get to know the real you. Don't try to be someone you're not, as this will likely come across as inauthentic and can negatively impact your chances of securing a role at the company. Instead, be confident in your abilities and showcase your personality, as this will help you to stand out from other candidates.

Practice Active Listening:

Active listening is a critical communication skill that is important to demonstrate during a Google interview. This means paying close attention to what the interviewer is saying, asking clarifying questions, and demonstrating that you are engaged in the conversation. Active listening shows that you are interested in the interviewer's perspective and demonstrates your ability to effectively communicate and collaborate with others.

Be Prepared to Ask Questions:

In addition to being an active listener, it's also important to be prepared to ask questions during the interview. This shows that you are engaged in the conversation and demonstrates your interest in the role and the company. Consider preparing a list of questions beforehand, including questions about the company's culture, the role you're applying for, and the team you'll be working with. Asking thoughtful questions can also help you to better understand the company and the role, which can be beneficial as you continue through the interview process.

Use Clear and Concise Language:

When communicating during a Google interview, it's important to use clear and concise language. This means avoiding technical jargon, using simple and straightforward language, and taking the time to explain complex concepts in a way that is easy to understand. Using clear and concise language demonstrates your ability to effectively communicate with a wide range of individuals, including those who may not have a technical background.

Showcase Your Communication Skills:

Google values individuals who have strong communication skills, as this is critical for success in a team-based environment. Be prepared to talk about your experience with effective communication, including your ability to work well with others, to provide feedback, and to resolve conflicts. Provide examples of situations where you have used your communication skills to achieve a desired outcome and discuss the impact of your efforts.

Demonstrate Your Positive Attitude:

Google values individuals who bring a positive attitude to the workplace, and it's important to showcase your positive attitude during the interview. This means being optimistic, enthusiastic, and approachable, and demonstrating a willingness to learn and grow. Show your positive attitude by speaking about your experiences in a positive light, focusing on the lessons you've learned, and discussing how you've used those lessons to improve your skills and experience.

Highlight Your Adaptability:

Google values individuals who are adaptable and able to adjust to change, and it's important to showcase this skill during the interview. Be prepared to talk about your experience with change, including how you've adapted to new technologies, new processes, or new teams. Discuss the challenges you've faced and how you've overcome them, and highlight your ability to work well in a fast-paced and dynamic environment.

In conclusion, effectively communicating and showcasing your personality during a Google interview is just as important as demonstrating your technical skills and experience. By being confident and authentic, practicing active listening, asking thoughtful questions, using clear and concise language, showcasing your communication skills, demonstrating a positive attitude, highlighting your adaptability, and emphasizing your collaboration skills, you can increase your chances of securing a role at Google. Remember to be yourself and bring your unique strengths to the interview, as this is what makes you stand out from other candidates. Good luck in your interview, and take the time to reflect on your experience, as this will help you to continue to grow and develop your skills.

Google is one of the world's leading technology companies, known for its innovative products and cutting-edge technology. The company has a strong presence in India, with multiple offices across the country and a large number of employees. In this article, we will explore how Google hires in India, including the company's recruitment process, the types of roles available, and the skills and qualifications required.

Recruitment Process:

Google's recruitment process in India typically consists of several stages, including an initial screening, a technical interview, and a final interview with the hiring manager. The initial screening typically involves submitting a resume and cover letter, and may include an online assessment of technical and problem-solving skills. The technical interview is a more in-depth conversation with a Google engineer, and is focused on evaluating the candidate's technical skills and experience. Finally, the final interview with the hiring manager is an opportunity to discuss the candidate's fit with the company and the role.

Types of Roles Available:

Google offers a wide range of roles in India, including positions in engineering, product management, sales, marketing, and more. Some of the most popular roles at Google include software engineer, product manager, data analyst, and user experience designer. The company is constantly evolving and growing, and new roles are added on a regular basis.

Required Skills and Qualifications:

Google is known for its rigorous recruitment process, and the company requires candidates to have strong technical skills, problem-solving abilities, and a passion for technology. The company values individuals who are creative, innovative, and have a strong work ethic. In addition to technical skills, Google also values individuals who have excellent communication and collaboration skills, as the company is focused on building a diverse and inclusive workplace.

Internships and Early Career Programs:

Google offers a range of internships and early career programs in India, designed to help students and recent graduates develop their skills and gain hands-on experience in their chosen field. These programs offer students the opportunity to work on real projects, gain mentorship from experienced professionals, and make connections within the industry. Participants in these programs also have the opportunity to receive feedback and coaching, and to network with other young professionals.

The Company Culture:

Google is known for its unique company culture, which is focused on collaboration, innovation, and a passion for technology. The company values individuals who are creative, curious, and driven, and who bring a positive attitude and a willingness to learn to the workplace. Google is also committed to diversity and inclusion, and the company values individuals from a wide range of backgrounds and perspectives.

Opportunities for Growth and Development:

Google offers a range of opportunities for growth and development, including training and development programs, mentorship opportunities, and the chance to work on cutting-edge technology. The company is committed to helping its employees grow and develop their skills, and encourages individuals to take on new challenges and explore new areas of interest.

Conclusion:

In conclusion, Google is a dynamic and innovative company with a strong presence in India. The company's recruitment process is rigorous and focused on evaluating technical skills, problem-solving abilities, and a passion for technology. Google offers a wide range of roles and opportunities for growth and development, and is committed to building a diverse and inclusive workplace. If you're interested in pursuing a career at Google, be sure to prepare for the recruitment process, showcase your skills and experience, and bring a positive attitude and a willingness to learn to the interview.

CHAPTER TEN

Understanding the Google technical interview and preparing for it with sample questions and solutions

The Google technical interview is known for being rigorous and challenging, but also a great opportunity to showcase your skills and knowledge. As a top technology company, Google is committed to hiring the best and brightest individuals, and the technical interview is an important part of this process. In this article, we'll take a closer look at what you can expect from the Google technical interview, and provide some tips and sample questions to help you prepare.

What to Expect:

The Google technical interview typically lasts between 45 minutes and an hour, and is focused on evaluating your technical skills, problem-solving abilities, and communication skills. During the interview, you'll be asked a series of technical questions and may be asked to write code or solve problems on a whiteboard. The interviewer will be looking for specific skills, including algorithms and data structures, programming, and systems design.

Tips for Preparation:

The key to success in the Google technical interview is preparation. Here are some tips to help you get ready:

Brush up on your algorithms and data structures: This is a critical area for the Google technical interview, and it's important to be familiar with the basics. Make sure you understand time and space complexity, sorting algorithms, and tree structures.

Practice coding: The Google technical interview often involves writing code, so it's important to practice your coding skills. You can use online resources, such as coding challenges and online forums, to improve your skills.

Study systems design: Systems design is a critical area in the Google technical interview, and it's important to understand how to design scalable and efficient systems. Make sure you're familiar with basic concepts, such as load balancing, caching, and databases.

Practice communication: The Google technical interview also involves evaluating your communication skills, so it's important to practice explaining complex technical concepts in a clear and concise way.

Sample Questions and Solutions:

To help you prepare for the Google technical interview, here are some sample questions and solutions:

Question: Given a string, write a function to check if it is a palindrome.

Solution: To solve this problem, you can write a function that takes a string as input and returns a Boolean value indicating whether the string is a palindrome or not. The function can use two pointers, one starting from the beginning of the string and the other from the end of the string, and compare the characters at each end. If all the characters match, the string is a palindrome.

Question: Design a system for tracking the most visited pages on a website.

Solution: To solve this problem, you can design a system that uses a hash table to store the URLs and their corresponding counts. The system can use a cache to store the most frequently visited pages, and update the cache whenever a page is visited. The cache can be updated in real-time, or on a regular basis, depending on the requirements.

Question: Given an array of integers, write a function to find the missing number.

Solution: To solve this problem, you can write a function that takes an array of integers as input and returns the missing number. The function can use a bit vector to store the presence or absence of each number in the array, and then find the missing number by checking which bit is not set.

Conclusion:

In conclusion, the Google technical interview is a rigorous and challenging process, but also a great opportunity to showcase your skills and knowledge. By preparing well, practicing your coding and communication skills, and studying algorithms and data structures, you can increase your chances of success in the interview.

Remember to stay calm

How to handle common interview challenges, such as stress, nervousness, and tough questions

Interviews can be nerve-wracking, especially when it's for a top technology company like Google. However, it's important to remember that interviews are also an opportunity to showcase your skills and demonstrate why you're a good fit for the company. To help you handle common interview challenges, such as stress, nervousness, and tough questions, this article provides tips and advice on how to prepare and perform at your best during a Google interview.

Tips for Handling Stress and Nervousness:

One of the biggest challenges during an interview is managing stress and nervousness. Here are some tips to help you stay calm and focused:

Practice deep breathing: Deep breathing can help you calm your nerves and improve your focus. Take a deep breath and hold it for a few seconds, then slowly release it. Repeat this several times before your interview.

Visualize your success: Visualization is a powerful technique for reducing stress and increasing confidence. Visualize yourself walking into the interview room, shaking hands with your interviewer, and confidently answering their questions.

Prepare in advance: Preparation is key to reducing stress and nervousness during an interview. Make sure you understand the company and the role you're applying for, and practice answering common interview questions.

Tips for Handling Tough Questions:

Tough questions can be a challenge during an interview, but they're also an opportunity to showcase your problem-solving skills and knowledge. Here are some tips for handling tough questions:

Take your time: Don't feel pressured to answer a tough question immediately. Take a moment to think about your answer and make sure you understand the question before you respond.

Ask for clarification: If you're unsure about a question, don't be afraid to ask for clarification. This shows that you're engaged and interested in the interview.

Be honest: If you don't know the answer to a question, it's better to be honest and admit it. You can then offer to research the answer or provide a different perspective on the topic.

Practice humility: Tough questions can be a chance to demonstrate your humility and willingness to learn. If you don't know the answer to a question, take it as an opportunity to show that you're always eager to learn and grow.

Tips for Showcasing Your Personality:

In addition to showcasing your technical skills, it's also important to let your personality shine during a Google interview. Here are some tips for demonstrating your personality:

Be yourself: The interview is an opportunity for the interviewer to get to know you, so don't try to be someone you're not. Be authentic and let your personality shine.

Show your passion: If you're passionate about a particular technology or project, let the interviewer know. This shows that you're engaged and invested in your work.

Ask questions: Don't be afraid to ask questions during the interview. This shows that you're interested in the company and the role, and gives you an opportunity to learn more about the company culture.

Conclusion:

In conclusion, the Google interview can be a challenging and nerve-wracking experience, but it's also an opportunity to showcase your skills and personality. By preparing in advance, staying calm, handling tough questions with confidence, and letting your personality shine, you can increase your chances of success during the interview. Remember, interviews are a two-way street, and the interviewer wants to get to know you as much as you want to get to know the company. So, relax, be yourself, and have fun!

CHAPTER TWELVE

The importance of follow-up after your interview and how to keep your momentum going

The interview process doesn't end once you leave the interview room. In fact, following up after the interview is just as important as the interview itself. It's a chance to reiterate your interest in the company and position, and to keep the momentum of the interview going. In this article, we'll explore the importance of follow-up after a Google interview and provide tips for keeping your momentum going.

Why Follow-Up is Important:

Follow-up after an interview serves several purposes:

Reinforces your interest: Following up after the interview shows that you're still interested in the company and the position, and reinforces your commitment to the role.

Provides an opportunity to address any concerns: If there were any areas of the interview that you felt you could have done better, following up provides an opportunity to address those concerns and showcase your problem-solving skills.

Builds relationships: Following up after the interview allows you to build relationships with the interviewer and the company, and can help you stand out from other candidates.

When to Follow-Up:

The timing of your follow-up is important. It's recommended to follow up within 24-48 hours of the interview. This shows that you're timely and proactive, and reinforces your interest in the role.

How to Follow-Up:

There are several ways to follow up after an interview:

Email: A thank-you email is a simple and effective way to follow up after an interview. Keep the email brief, professional, and to the point, and reiterate your interest in the role.

Phone call: If you prefer a more personal touch, you can follow up with a phone call. This allows you to have a more direct conversation with the interviewer, and provides an opportunity to ask any questions you may have.

LinkedIn: Following up through LinkedIn can help you maintain a professional connection with the interviewer and the company, and can also serve as a platform for future communication.

Keeping the Momentum Going:

Once you've followed up, it's important to keep the momentum going. Here are some tips for keeping the momentum of your interview going:

Stay organized: Keep track of your interviews, follow-up activities, and any notes from the interview. This will help you stay organized and ensure that you don't miss any important details.

Stay engaged: Continue to research the company and stay engaged with the interviewer and the company. This shows that you're still interested in the role, and helps you build relationships.

Stay positive: Maintain a positive attitude and remain confident in your abilities. Remember, rejection is not a reflection of your worth or abilities, and there will always be other opportunities.

Conclusion:

In conclusion, following up after a Google interview is an important step in the interview process. By following up promptly, building relationships, and keeping the momentum going, you can increase your chances of success and stand out from other candidates. Remember, the interview process is a two-way street, and following up is an opportunity to demonstrate your commitment and interest in the role. So, stay organized, stay engaged, and stay positive, and you'll be well on your way to landing your dream job at Google!

CHAPTER THIRTEEN

Understanding the Google offer process and what to expect after your interview

The Google offer process is an exciting and potentially life-changing experience, but it can also be a stressful and confusing journey. After spending weeks or even months preparing for the interview and going through the different stages of the hiring process, you might be left wondering what happens next and what to expect if you are offered a job.

In this article, we will walk you through the different stages of the Google offer process, from the moment you receive the offer to your first day on the job. We will cover what to expect, how to negotiate your offer, and what to do if you receive multiple offers. We will also explore some of the perks and benefits of working at Google, as well as the challenges and responsibilities that come with the job.

Receiving the Offer

The first step in the Google offer process is receiving the offer itself. After you have successfully completed the interview process and the hiring committee has made a decision, you will receive an email or phone call from a recruiter with the good news.

The offer will include details such as your salary, benefits, and start date, as well as information about any stock options or bonuses that may be included. It is important to review the offer carefully and make sure you understand all the terms and conditions.

If you are happy with the offer, you can accept it by replying to the recruiter and confirming your start date. If you have any questions or concerns, you can also discuss them with the recruiter and ask for clarification.

Negotiating Your Offer

If you are not satisfied with the offer or if you think you are worth more than what has been offered, you can try to negotiate your offer. Google is known for offering competitive compensation packages, but it is still possible to negotiate for a higher salary, more stock options, or better benefits.

When negotiating your offer, it is important to be professional and respectful. Explain your reasons for wanting to negotiate and provide evidence to support your case. You can also ask the recruiter for their opinion on the matter and see if they are willing to work with you to find a solution that works for both parties.

It is important to keep in mind that negotiations are not always successful, and that pushing too hard can sometimes backfire. If you are not happy with the final offer, you can still decline the offer and continue your job search.

Dealing with Multiple Offers

If you are lucky enough to receive multiple job offers, it can be both exciting and overwhelming. It is important to carefully consider each offer and weigh the pros and cons of each company and role.

When comparing offers, it is important to consider factors such as salary, benefits, location, company culture, and growth opportunities. You can also reach out to people in your network or online communities to get their opinions and advice.

If you decide to go with Google, you can politely decline the other offers and notify the recruiters of your decision. It is important to do this as soon as possible to avoid leaving the other companies hanging and to maintain a professional reputation.

Preparing for Your First Day

After accepting the offer and negotiating any final details, it is time to prepare for your first day on the job. This can be a nerve-wracking experience, but it is also an exciting opportunity to start a new chapter in your career.

Before your first day, you should familiarize yourself with Google's culture and values, as well as the specific team and project you will be working on. You can also reach out to your manager or team lead to introduce yourself and ask any questions you may have.

It is also important to prepare yourself mentally and emotionally for the challenges and responsibilities that come with the job. Working at Google can be demanding and fast-paced, but it is also a rewarding and fulfilling experience.

CHAPTER FOURTEEN

Staying motivated and confident throughout the job search process, regardless of the outcome

Searching for a job can be a long and challenging process that can take a toll on your motivation and confidence. The ups and downs of job searching can be emotionally draining, but it is important to stay motivated and confident throughout the process, regardless of the outcome.

In this article, we will discuss some tips and strategies for staying motivated and confident during the job search process. We will explore ways to manage stress, maintain a positive mindset, and set realistic goals. We will also discuss how to deal with rejection and failure, and how to stay focused on your long-term career goals.

Managing Stress

Job searching can be a stressful and overwhelming process, but it is important to manage that stress in healthy ways. One way to manage stress is to set boundaries and schedule breaks throughout your day. This will allow you to recharge and refocus your energy, and help you avoid burnout.

Another way to manage stress is to practice self-care activities, such as exercise, meditation, or spending time with loved ones. These activities can help reduce stress levels and increase feelings of well-being and positivity.

Maintaining a Positive Mindset

Maintaining a positive mindset is important when job searching. This can be challenging when faced with rejection or setbacks, but it is crucial to stay optimistic and focus on the positive aspects of the job search process.

One way to maintain a positive mindset is to focus on your strengths and achievements. Write down your accomplishments, and review them regularly to remind yourself of your worth and capabilities.

Another way to maintain a positive mindset is to visualize your goals and the outcomes you want to achieve. This can help you stay motivated and focused on your long-term career goals.

Setting Realistic Goals

Setting realistic goals is important when job searching. It is important to set achievable goals that can be measured and evaluated, and to break them down into smaller, manageable tasks.

It is also important to be flexible and adaptable when setting goals. Be open to adjusting your goals and strategies as needed, based on new information and feedback.

Dealing with Rejection and Failure

Dealing with rejection and failure is a natural part of the job search process, but it can be discouraging and demotivating. It is important to remember that rejection and failure are not a reflection of your worth or abilities, but rather an opportunity to learn and grow.

One way to deal with rejection and failure is to reflect on what you can learn from the experience. Ask for feedback and advice from recruiters or hiring managers, and use that feedback to improve your skills and approach.

Another way to deal with rejection and failure is to stay positive and keep moving forward. Don't dwell on the past, but rather focus on the present and the future. Keep applying to new opportunities and stay open to new possibilities.

Staying Focused on Long-Term Career Goals

Staying focused on your long-term career goals is important when job searching. It is important to keep in mind the big picture and the direction you want your career to go, even if the job search process is taking longer than expected.

One way to stay focused on your long-term career goals is to set milestones and celebrate your progress along the way. This can help you stay motivated and focused on the end goal.

Another way to stay focused on your long-term career goals is to network and connect with other professionals in your field. Attend industry events, join online communities, and reach out to mentors or advisors for guidance and support.

Conclusion

Staying motivated and confident throughout the job search process is not always easy, but it is crucial for success. By managing stress, maintaining a positive mindset, setting realistic goals, dealing with rejection and failure, and staying focused on your long-term career goals, you can stay motivated and confident, regardless of the outcome.

• 57 •

CHAPTER FIFTEEN

Different Jobs at Google

Google is one of the most prestigious and innovative companies in the world, known for its cutting-edge technology, dynamic culture, and highly talented workforce. With a range of job opportunities spanning from engineering to marketing, from human resources to product management, there is a job at Google for almost anyone who is looking for a challenging and rewarding career.

In this article, we will explore the different types of jobs available at Google, the skills and qualifications required for each position, and the responsibilities and benefits of working at Google.

Engineering Jobs

Google is renowned for its engineering prowess, and it is one of the top destinations for software developers, data analysts, and other technical professionals. Here are some of the engineering jobs available at Google:

Software Engineer - Software engineers at Google are responsible for designing, developing, and testing software applications and systems, ranging from mobile apps to search algorithms. They work closely with product managers and other stakeholders to ensure that the software meets the needs of users and business requirements.

Data Scientist - Data scientists at Google analyze large amounts of data to identify patterns, trends, and insights that can help the company make better decisions. They use statistical models, machine learning algorithms, and other data analysis techniques to extract meaningful information from vast data sets.

Network Engineer - Network engineers at Google are responsible for designing, building, and maintaining the company's network infrastructure, including servers, routers, and other hardware components. They ensure that the network is secure, reliable, and scalable, and they troubleshoot any issues that arise.

Marketing and Sales Jobs

Google's marketing and sales teams are responsible for promoting and selling the company's products and services to customers around the world. Here are some of the marketing and sales jobs available at Google:

Marketing Manager - Marketing managers at Google develop and execute marketing campaigns that increase brand awareness, generate leads, and drive sales. They work closely with product managers and sales teams to create messaging that resonates with customers, and they use data and analytics to measure the effectiveness of marketing programs.

Account Manager - Account managers at Google are responsible for building relationships with clients, understanding their needs, and providing them with solutions that meet their business goals. They work with cross-functional teams to ensure that the client's needs are met, and they provide ongoing support to ensure customer satisfaction.

Sales Engineer - Sales engineers at Google are technical experts who work with sales teams to explain the benefits of Google's products and services to customers. They use their technical knowledge to explain how Google's solutions can help customers solve their business challenges, and they work with engineering teams to develop custom solutions that meet specific customer needs.

Product Management Jobs

Product managers at Google are responsible for creating and managing products that solve customer needs and drive business growth. They work with cross-functional teams to define product strategy, develop product roadmaps, and launch products to market. Here are some of the product management jobs available at Google:

Product Manager - Product managers at Google are responsible for defining the vision and strategy for their products, and they work with cross-functional teams to bring those products to market. They use customer feedback, market research, and data analysis to inform their product decisions, and they collaborate with engineering and design teams to build products that meet user needs.

Technical Program Manager - Technical program managers at Google are responsible for managing the development and launch of complex software products. They work with engineering teams to define project requirements, develop project plans, and ensure that projects are delivered on time and within budget.

UX Designer - UX designers at Google are responsible for creating user interfaces that are intuitive, engaging, and easy to use.

Other Jobs at Google

In addition to the jobs listed above, there are many other job opportunities available at Google, ranging from human resources to finance to operations. Here are some examples:

Human Resources Manager - Human resources managers at Google are responsible for attracting and retaining top talent, as well as developing programs and policies that support the company's culture and values.

Financial Analyst - Financial analysts at Google are responsible for analyzing financial data and providing insights that support business decision-making. They work with cross-functional teams to identify areas of opportunity and create financial forecasts and budgets.

Program Manager - Program managers at Google are responsible for managing complex projects that involve multiple teams and stakeholders. They work with cross-functional teams to develop project plans, track progress, and ensure that projects are completed on time and within budget.

Working at Google

Working at Google is a dream for many professionals, and for good reason. The company is known for its employee-friendly culture, generous benefits, and commitment to innovation. Here are some of the benefits of working at Google:

Competitive Salary - Google offers competitive salaries that are based on experience, skills, and performance.

Generous Benefits - Google offers a range of benefits to its employees, including health insurance, retirement plans, and wellness programs.

Culture of Innovation - Google is known for its culture of innovation, and employees are encouraged to experiment, take risks, and think creatively.

Conclusion

In conclusion, there are many different job opportunities available at Google, ranging from engineering to marketing to product management. Each job requires different skills and qualifications, but they all share a commitment to innovation, creativity, and a customer-centric approach.

Working at Google is a rewarding experience that offers many benefits, including competitive salaries, generous benefits, and a culture of innovation. If you are interested in pursuing a career at Google, be sure to research the job opportunities that are available and find a role that aligns with your skills, interests, and career goals.

CHAPTER SIXTEEN

A Day in the Life of a Googler

The life of a Googler is often seen as a dream job for many people. Working for one of the largest and most innovative companies in the world, Googlers get to work on cutting-edge technologies, collaborate with some of the brightest minds in the industry, and enjoy a range of perks and benefits. But what does it really mean to be a Googler, and what does a typical day in the life of a Googler look like?

The Culture of Google

Google is known for its unique and employee-friendly culture. The company's mission statement is to "organize the world's information and make it universally accessible and useful," and this mission is reflected in everything that the company does, from its products and services to its employee culture.

At Google, employees are encouraged to think creatively, take risks, and experiment. This culture of innovation is what has made Google one of the most successful companies in the world, and it is also what makes working at Google such a rewarding experience.

A Day in the Life of a Googler

So what does a typical day in the life of a Googler look like? While the specifics vary depending on the role and team, here is a general overview of what a day in the life of a Googler might entail:

Morning: Many Googlers start their day with a visit to the company's on-site gym or fitness center. Exercise and wellness are an important part of Google's culture, and the company provides a range of fitness and wellness programs to its employees.

After arriving at the office, a Googler might attend a team meeting or check in with their manager to discuss project priorities for the day. Collaboration and communication are key parts of the job at Google, and employees are encouraged to work closely with their colleagues to achieve their goals.

During the day: Throughout the day, a Googler might spend time coding or designing new products, attending meetings or brainstorming sessions, or conducting research and data analysis. Google provides its employees with the latest tools and technologies to help them be as productive and innovative as possible.

Afternoon: Many Googlers take a break in the afternoon to enjoy some of the company's on-site amenities, such as the cafes or game rooms. This is a great opportunity to socialize with colleagues, take a mental break, and recharge for the rest of the day.

Evening: The work day at Google typically ends around 6PM, but some Googlers may work longer hours depending on project deadlines and priorities. After work, Googlers might attend company-sponsored events, such as guest speakers or networking sessions, or head home to spend time with family or pursue personal interests.

Benefits of Being a Googler

One of the biggest draws of working at Google is the range of perks and benefits that the company offers to its employees. Here are just a few of the benefits that Googlers can enjoy:

Competitive salary: Google offers competitive salaries that are based on experience, skills, and performance.

Generous benefits: Googlers receive a range of benefits, including health insurance, retirement plans, and wellness programs.

On-site amenities: Google provides on-site cafes, gyms, and game rooms to help employees stay healthy and engaged.

Professional development: Googlers have access to a range of professional development opportunities, including training programs and conferences.

Conclusion

In conclusion, the life of a Googler is both rewarding and challenging. Working at one of the most innovative and successful companies in the world offers many benefits, but it also requires a high level of skill, creativity, and dedication. If you are interested in pursuing a career at Google, be sure to research the different job opportunities that are available, and find a role that align

CHAPTER SEVENTEEN

Life of Noogler's

The life of a "Noogler" - a new employee at Google - can be both exciting and overwhelming. Starting a new job can be a daunting experience, but starting at one of the most innovative and fast-paced companies in the world can be even more challenging. So what is life like for a Noogler, and how can new employees make the most of their time at Google?

The Onboarding Process

The onboarding process at Google is designed to help new employees get up to speed as quickly as possible. The process typically lasts for a few weeks and includes a range of training and orientation programs. During this time, Nooglers will have the opportunity to learn about the company's culture, values, and processes, as well as the specifics of their job role.

Nooglers will also be assigned a buddy or mentor, who is typically a more experienced employee at Google. The buddy will be responsible for helping the Noogler navigate the company culture, answer questions, and provide guidance and support.

A Typical Day as a Noogler

A typical day as a Noogler will vary depending on the role and team, but here is a general overview of what a day might entail:

Morning: Nooglers may start their day with a visit to the company's on-site gym or fitness center. Exercise and wellness are an important part of Google's culture, and the company provides a range of fitness and wellness programs to its employees.

After arriving at the office, a Noogler may attend a team meeting or check in with their manager to discuss project priorities for the day. Collaboration and communication are key parts of the job at Google, and Nooglers are encouraged to work closely with their colleagues to achieve their goals.

During the day: Throughout the day, a Noogler may spend time coding or designing new products, attending meetings or brainstorming sessions, or conducting research and data analysis. Google provides its employees with the latest tools and technologies to help them be as productive and innovative as possible.

Afternoon: Many Nooglers take a break in the afternoon to enjoy some of the company's on-site amenities, such as the cafes or game rooms. This is a great opportunity to socialize with colleagues, take a mental break, and recharge for the rest of the day.

Evening: The work day at Google typically ends around 6PM, but some Nooglers may work longer hours depending on project deadlines and priorities. After work, Nooglers may attend company-sponsored events, such as guest speakers or networking sessions, or head home to spend time with family or pursue personal interests.

Challenges and Opportunities

Starting a new job at Google can be both exciting and challenging. Nooglers may face a range of challenges, including adjusting to a fast-paced and constantly changing work environment, learning new technologies and tools, and building relationships with colleagues.

However, there are also many opportunities for growth and development as a Noogler. Google offers a range of training and development programs, as well as opportunities to work on high-impact projects and collaborate with some of the brightest minds in the industry.

Tips for Success as a Noogler

Here are a few tips for success as a Noogler:

Embrace the culture: Google has a unique and employee-friendly culture, so take the time to learn about the company's values and processes, and try to embrace them as much as possible.

Ask questions: Don't be afraid to ask questions and seek help when needed. Your buddy or mentor, as well as your colleagues, are there to support you and help you succeed.

Be open to learning: The pace of innovation at Google is fast, and there will always be new technologies and tools to learn.

CHAPTER EIGHTEEN

Google's Onboarding Process

Joining Google as a new employee, also known as a "Noogler," can be an exciting and nerve-wracking experience. While the company's reputation precedes itself in terms of its unique work culture, top-notch benefits, and cutting-edge technology, the onboarding process can feel like a maze. This guide is designed to give you a comprehensive overview of the Google onboarding process and everything you need to know to make the most of your welcome kit.

Section 1: Before You Start at Google

Preparing for your role

What to expect from your hiring manager and the recruiting team

Preparing for your move (if applicable)

Section 2: Day One: Orientation

Introduction to the Google culture and values

Meeting your peers and team members

Tour of the campus and facilities

Information about company policies, procedures, and benefits

Section 3: The First Few Weeks: Training and Team Building

Overview of training programs

Opportunities for skill-building and professional development

Building relationships with your team and colleagues

Understanding your role and responsibilities

Section 4: Your Welcome Kit: What You'll Receive and How to Use It

A detailed look at the contents of the welcome kit

How to set up your equipment and get started with the software

Best practices for using your new Google tools and technology

Tips for organizing and customizing your workspace

Section 5: Making the Most of Your Onboarding Experience

Tips for staying organized and on top of your tasks

Strategies for building relationships and integrating with your team

Making the most of your training opportunities

Taking advantage of Google's unique culture and benefits

Section 6: Conclusion

Reflecting on your onboarding experience

Planning for your future at Google

Tips for helping new hires in the future

Conclusion: Google's onboarding process is designed to set new employees up for success and ensure a smooth transition into the company culture. By understanding what to expect and how to make the most of your welcome kit, you can hit the ground running and start contributing to the team right away. Remember to stay organized, build relationships, and take advantage of the many training opportunities and benefits that Google offers. Good luck on your new adventure as a Noogler!

• 71 •

CHAPTER NINETEEN

The launch of the Google search engine and its reception

The launch of the Google search engine in 1998 was a turning point in the history of the internet. Developed by Larry Page and Sergey Brin, two computer science students at Stanford University, Google used a unique approach to web search that revolutionized the way people found information online.

At the time of its launch, Google was just one of many search engines vying for users' attention. But the company's approach, which relied on a complex algorithm called PageRank to determine the relevance of web pages, quickly set it apart from the competition.

Google's simple and uncluttered interface, which featured a single search box and a logo in primary colors, was also a departure from the crowded and cluttered interfaces of other search engines. It was fast, intuitive, and easy to use, and users quickly began to gravitate towards it.

Within a few years of its launch, Google had become the most popular search engine on the internet, with more than 70% of the search market share. It had also become a cultural phenomenon, with its name becoming a verb synonymous with web search.

Part of the reason for Google's success was its focus on relevance and accuracy. Unlike other search engines of the time, Google's PageRank algorithm took into account not just the quantity of links pointing to a website but also the relevance of the content on the site. This made it much more effective at delivering useful search results to users.

Google's launch was met with enthusiasm and praise from users and tech experts alike. Its simple and intuitive interface, along with its accurate and relevant search results, made it an instant hit. The company's focus on user experience and simplicity also helped it win over users who were frustrated with the cluttered and confusing interfaces of other search engines.

Over the years, Google continued to refine its search algorithms and add new features, such as personalized search results and local search. The company also diversified into a wide range of other businesses, including cloud computing, advertising, and artificial intelligence.

Today, Google is one of the most valuable companies in the world, with a market capitalization of over $1 trillion. Its search engine handles billions of searches every day, and the company continues to innovate and push the boundaries of what's possible on the internet.

In conclusion, the launch of the Google search engine in 1998 was a watershed moment in the history of the internet. Its unique approach to web search, its simple and intuitive interface, and its focus on relevance and accuracy helped it win over users and quickly become the most popular search engine in the world. Google's impact on the internet and on the way we find information is immeasurable, and its legacy continues to be felt to this day.

Early competition with other search engines

When Google was founded in 1998, it faced stiff competition from several other search engines that were already established in the market. These included Yahoo!, AltaVista, and Excite, among others. Despite the competition, Google's unique approach to search quickly set it apart from the pack.

At the time, most search engines relied on keyword matching to deliver results. This meant that the search engine would look for the specific words entered by the user and return results that contained those words. However, this approach often resulted in irrelevant or low-quality search results.

Google's founders, Larry Page and Sergey Brin, took a different approach. They developed a complex algorithm called PageRank, which used links between web pages as a way of measuring the importance and relevance of a page. In other words, the more links a page had from other pages, the more important it was deemed to be.

This approach allowed Google to deliver more accurate and relevant search results than its competitors. Users quickly took notice, and Google's popularity began to grow.

In 1999, the company reached a milestone when it handled 500,000 searches in a single day.

Despite its growing popularity, Google still faced challenges from other search engines. Yahoo!, which was one of the most popular search engines at the time, even tried to acquire Google in 2002. However, Google's founders declined the offer, and the company continued to grow on its own.

Over time, Google's approach to search and its focus on user experience helped it win over users who were frustrated with the cluttered and confusing interfaces of other search engines. By the early 2000s, Google had surpassed all of its competitors to become the most popular search engine in the world.

In conclusion, Google's early competition with other search engines was fierce, but its unique approach to search and its focus on relevance and accuracy helped it stand out. By prioritizing user experience and delivering accurate search results, Google quickly won over users and became the most popular search engine in the world. Today, it remains one of the most valuable companies in the world, and its impact on the internet and on the way we find information is immeasurable.

CHAPTER TWENTY-ONE

Expansion into new areas, such as email and maps

Since its founding in 1998, Google has expanded beyond its origins as a search engine to become one of the most diversified and innovative companies in the world. In addition to its core search business, the company has launched a wide range of products and services in areas such as email, maps, and mobile operating systems.

One of Google's earliest expansions was into email with the launch of Gmail in 2004. At the time, email was dominated by services such as Yahoo! Mail and Hotmail, but Google's entry into the market brought a new level of innovation and user experience. With features such as threaded conversations, labels, and powerful search capabilities, Gmail quickly became one of the most popular email services in the world.

Another major expansion for Google was in the area of maps. In 2005, the company launched Google Maps, which offered a new level of detail and interactivity compared to existing online maps. With features such as street view, satellite imagery, and real-time traffic updates, Google Maps quickly became the go-to service for anyone looking for directions or exploring a new area.

Google has also made major strides in the mobile space with its Android operating system, which was launched in 2008. Android has since become the most popular mobile operating system in the world, powering billions of devices worldwide. In addition to its core operating system, Google has also launched a wide range of mobile apps and services, including Google Maps, Gmail, and Google Assistant.

Other areas of expansion for Google include cloud computing, artificial intelligence, and self-driving cars. The company's cloud platform, Google Cloud, is now one of the largest cloud computing providers in the world, with a wide range of services for businesses and developers. Google's focus on artificial intelligence has also led to major breakthroughs in areas such as natural language processing, image recognition, and machine learning.

In conclusion, Google's expansion into new areas such as email, maps, and mobile operating systems has been a key driver of the company's success. With a focus on innovation and user experience, Google has been able to launch a wide range of products and services that have become integral parts of our daily lives. As the company continues to expand into new areas, it will be interesting to see what new breakthroughs and innovations it will bring to the world.

CHAPTER TWENTY-TWO

The development of the AdWords platform and the introduction of online advertising

In the early days of the internet, online advertising was a relatively new and untested field. But with the growth of the web and the increasing popularity of search engines like Google, a new era of online advertising began. In this article, we will explore the development of Google's AdWords platform, which revolutionized online advertising and helped to make Google one of the most valuable companies in the world.

The Early Days of Online Advertising

In the early days of the web, online advertising was a relatively simple affair. Advertisers would purchase banner ads or other display advertising on popular websites, with the hope of reaching a broad audience. However, this approach had several drawbacks. For one thing, it was difficult to measure the effectiveness of these ads, as there was no easy way to track how many people were actually clicking on them.

The introduction of search engines like Google changed this equation. Suddenly, advertisers had a new way to reach potential customers. Rather than relying on display advertising, they could target people who were actively searching for products or services related to their business. This new approach, known as search advertising, quickly became popular, and search engines like Google began to make significant investments in this area.

The Birth of AdWords

In 2000, Google launched AdWords, its new search advertising platform. AdWords was designed to give advertisers more control over their ad campaigns and provide them with detailed metrics on the performance of their ads. With AdWords, advertisers could choose which keywords they wanted to target and set a budget for their ad campaigns.

One of the key innovations of AdWords was its use of a pay-per-click (PPC) model. With PPC, advertisers only pay when someone clicks on their ad, rather than paying a set fee for a certain number of impressions. This meant that advertisers could be more confident that they were getting value for their ad spend, as they only paid for clicks that actually led to potential customers.

The Rise of Keyword Advertising

One of the keys to AdWords' success was its focus on keyword advertising. With keyword advertising, advertisers could target people who were actively searching for products or services related to their business. For example, a business selling running shoes could target keywords like "running shoes" or "best running shoes." This approach allowed advertisers to reach a highly targeted audience, increasing the likelihood that they would convert to customers.

AdWords also introduced the concept of Quality Score, which is a metric that Google uses to measure the relevance and usefulness of an ad. Quality Score is based on factors such as the relevance of the ad to the search query, the quality of the landing page, and the historical performance of the ad. Ads with a higher Quality Score are more likely to be shown to users, and advertisers with higher Quality Scores are able to get more clicks for less money.

The Introduction of AdSense

In addition to AdWords, Google also launched AdSense, a complementary platform that allowed website owners to display ads on their sites and earn revenue from clicks. With AdSense, Google was able to extend its reach even further, as advertisers could now target people who were browsing popular websites rather than just searching on Google. AdSense quickly became popular with website owners, as it offered a new way to monetize their traffic.

The Evolution of AdWords

Over the years, AdWords has continued to evolve, with Google introducing a range of new features and tools to help advertisers get the most out of their ad campaigns. For example, in 2005, Google launched the AdWords API, which allows third-party developers to build applications that integrate with AdWords. This has led to a wide range of third-party tools and services that help advertisers to manage their campaigns more efficiently.

CHAPTER TWENTY-THREE

The acquisition of other companies and integration of their technology

In the highly competitive tech industry, companies like Google are constantly looking for ways to innovate and stay ahead of the game. One strategy that Google has employed over the years is the acquisition of other companies and integration of their technology into their own products and services.

Google's history of acquisitions dates back to 2001 with the purchase of Deja.com. Since then, Google has acquired over 200 companies, ranging from small startups to large corporations, including YouTube, Android, and Nest. These acquisitions have enabled Google to expand its capabilities and stay at the forefront of technological innovation.

The integration of acquired technologies into Google's products has been a key part of their strategy. For example, Google's acquisition of Android in 2005 allowed the company to enter the mobile operating system market and compete with Apple's iOS. Today, Android is the most popular mobile operating system in the world, powering over 2.5 billion devices globally.

Google's acquisition of YouTube in 2006 has also been a major success story. The video-sharing platform has become a staple of online entertainment, with over 2 billion monthly active users. Google has integrated YouTube into its suite of products, allowing users to easily access and share videos across multiple platforms.

Another notable acquisition by Google was Nest in 2014. Nest's smart home technology, including thermostats and security cameras, was integrated into Google's own smart home ecosystem, Google Home. This acquisition allowed Google to enter the growing smart home market and compete with other tech giants like Amazon and Apple.

While Google's acquisition strategy has been successful, it has also faced scrutiny from regulators and competitors. Google has been accused of using acquisitions to stifle competition and strengthen its market dominance. In 2020, the US Department of Justice filed a lawsuit against Google, alleging that the company had used its acquisitions to maintain a monopoly in the search and advertising markets.

Despite the challenges, the acquisition of other companies and integration of their technology has been a key part of Google's success. It has enabled the company to expand its capabilities, enter new markets, and stay at the forefront of technological innovation. As the tech industry continues to evolve, it will be interesting to see how Google's acquisition strategy evolves as well.

CHAPTER TWENTY-FOUR

The launch of new products, such as Google Drive and Google+

The launch of new products is a crucial aspect of any tech company's growth strategy, and Google is no exception. Over the years, Google has launched a range of products and services, some of which have become household names. Two notable examples are Google Drive and Google+.

Google Drive, launched in 2012, is a cloud-based storage and collaboration platform that allows users to store and share files and documents online. The platform offers a range of features, including real-time collaboration, version control, and powerful search capabilities. Google Drive was designed to compete with other cloud storage services such as Dropbox and Microsoft's OneDrive.

One of the key selling points of Google Drive is its integration with other Google products such as Google Docs, Sheets, and Slides. This integration allows users to easily create, edit, and share documents within Google Drive, making it a popular choice for individuals and businesses alike. Today, Google Drive has over 1 billion active users and has become a critical tool for productivity and collaboration.

Google+ was launched in 2011 as a social networking platform designed to compete with Facebook. The platform was designed to be more privacy-focused, with features such as Circles, which allowed users to group their contacts into different categories and share content with specific groups of people.

Despite its unique features, Google+ struggled to gain traction and compete with Facebook. The platform was eventually shut down in 2019, with Google citing low usage and engagement as the primary reasons for its closure. While Google+ was not a success, it did pave the way for other social networking platforms like Google Meet and Google Chat.

The launch of new products is not without its challenges. For example, Google+ faced a range of issues, including privacy concerns and a lack of user adoption. Similarly, the launch of Google Glass, a wearable technology that offered a range of features such as hands-free photography and voice recognition, faced criticism and concerns about privacy and safety.

Despite these challenges, the launch of new products is a critical component of Google's growth strategy. It allows the company to stay at the forefront of technological innovation and expand its capabilities into new markets. In recent years, Google has launched a range of new products, including Google Assistant, Google Home, and the Pixel smartphone.

The success of these products has varied, with some, such as the Pixel, gaining a loyal following, while others, such as Google Stadia, a cloud-based gaming platform, failing to gain traction.

In conclusion, the launch of new products is a key part of Google's growth strategy. While not every product will be a success, the company's ability to innovate and develop new products has enabled it to expand its capabilities and stay at the forefront of technological innovation. With the tech industry continuing to evolve at a rapid pace, it will be interesting to see what new products and services Google will launch in the future.

In conclusion, Google Drive and Google+ are two notable products launched by Google, each with its own unique features and capabilities. While Google Drive has become a critical tool for productivity and collaboration, Google+ faced challenges and eventually shut down. Despite its struggles, Google+ paved the way for other social networking and messaging platforms, which have become increasingly popular in recent years. As the tech industry continues to evolve, it will be interesting to see what new products and services Google will launch in the future.

CHAPTER TWENTY-FIVE

Google APM

Google is one of the world's most recognizable technology companies, known for its innovative products and services that have revolutionized the way we live, work, and communicate. One of the keys to Google's success is its team of talented product managers who are responsible for driving innovation, building successful products, and delivering value to customers.

Google APM, or Associate Product Manager, is a highly competitive program that aims to train the next generation of product managers at Google. This program is designed to provide recent graduates with the skills, knowledge, and experience needed to become successful product managers in one of the world's most dynamic and challenging technology companies.

In this article, we'll explore what Google APM is, how it works, and what you need to do to become a product manager at Google.

Section 1: What is Google APM? In this section, we'll provide an overview of what Google APM is, its history, and its purpose. We'll also discuss what makes Google APM unique and why it's one of the most competitive and prestigious programs in the tech industry.

Section 2: How Does Google APM Work? In this section, we'll dive into the details of how the Google APM program works. We'll explore the application process, what the program entails, and what you can expect if you're accepted into the program. We'll also discuss the structure of the program and what you'll be working on as an APM.

Section 3: What Skills and Qualifications Are Required for Google APM? In this section, we'll outline the skills and qualifications you'll need to be considered for the Google APM program. We'll explore the educational requirements, the skills and experience needed, and the qualities that Google looks for in its APMs. We'll also provide tips on how to improve your chances of being accepted into the program.

Section 4: What Are the Benefits of Google APM? In this section, we'll discuss the benefits of participating in the Google APM program. We'll explore the opportunities for professional growth, the exposure to cutting-edge technology and industry trends, and the potential for career advancement. We'll also discuss the compensation and benefits package for Google APMs.

Section 5: What Happens After Google APM? In this section, we'll explore what happens after you complete the Google APM program. We'll discuss the potential career paths for APMs at Google, including the possibility of becoming a full-time product manager. We'll also discuss the opportunities to work in other areas of the tech industry and the potential for continued professional growth and development.

Section 6: Tips for Success in the Google APM Program In this section, we'll provide tips and advice for succeeding in the Google APM program. We'll discuss how to stand out during the application process, what to expect during the program, and how to make the most of your time as an APM. We'll also discuss the importance of networking and building relationships with other APMs and product managers at Google.

Conclusion: Google APM is a highly competitive program that offers recent graduates the opportunity to become product managers at one of the world's most innovative and successful technology companies. If you're interested in pursuing a career in product management, Google APM is an excellent way to get your foot in the door and gain the skills, knowledge, and experience needed to succeed in this exciting and challenging field. With the information and tips provided in this article, you'll be well on your way to becoming a product manager at Google.

CHAPTER TWENTY-SIX

The Tech Titans Face-Off: Google vs Microsoft vs Apple

In recent years, Google has been at the forefront of technological innovation, driving major advancements in artificial intelligence (AI), cloud computing, and machine learning. Through its subsidiary companies such as Waymo and DeepMind, Google has also been making significant strides in the fields of autonomous vehicles and healthcare.

One of Google's key strengths is its dominance in the search engine market, with its search engine being the most widely used in the world. However, the company's ambitions go far beyond search, with a focus on developing and improving a wide range of technologies, such as Google Drive, Google Maps, and Google Assistant.

In the area of AI and machine learning, Google has been investing heavily in developing new algorithms and models that are designed to improve the performance of its search engine and other products. The company has also been using these technologies to develop new products, such as Google Duplex, which is an AI-powered virtual assistant that can carry out tasks like making reservations or scheduling appointments.

Google is also heavily focused on cloud computing, with its cloud services platform, Google Cloud Platform (GCP), competing directly with other tech giants like Amazon Web Services (AWS) and Microsoft Azure. The company has been investing heavily in expanding its data center infrastructure to support the growing demand for cloud services.

One of the most ambitious projects that Google is working on is Waymo, its self-driving car subsidiary. Waymo has been developing autonomous vehicles for several years and has been testing its technology in a number of cities across the United States. The company has also partnered with automakers like Fiat Chrysler to develop self-driving cars that can be used for ride-sharing services.

In the healthcare industry, Google has been making significant strides in the area of disease detection and diagnosis. Through its subsidiary, DeepMind, the company has been developing algorithms that can analyze medical images and help doctors identify potential health issues. The company has also been using machine learning to analyze large sets of medical data in order to identify patterns and potential health risks.

Despite its many successes, Google faces challenges in a number of areas, including data privacy, antitrust issues, and regulatory hurdles. The company has been the subject of several high-profile antitrust investigations in recent years, with regulators in Europe and the United States questioning the company's business practices and market dominance.

Overall, Google remains a major force in the tech industry, pushing the boundaries of what is possible through its many innovative products and services. While it faces challenges and competition from other tech giants, the company's focus on innovation, collaboration, and investment in emerging technologies puts it in a strong position to continue shaping the future of technology.

The tech industry is dominated by a few major players who are constantly competing with each other to push the limits of innovation and bring new products and services to market. Three of the biggest players in this space are Google, Microsoft, and Apple. These companies have been competing with each other for decades, each with its own unique strengths and weaknesses. In this article, we'll take a closer look at how these tech titans stack up against each other.

Section 1: Google In this section, we'll take a closer look at Google, its history, and its place in the tech industry. We'll explore Google's strengths and weaknesses, including its search engine dominance, its focus on data and AI, and its challenges with data privacy and antitrust issues.

Section 2: Microsoft In this section, we'll explore Microsoft's history, its strengths and weaknesses, and how it has evolved over the years. We'll discuss Microsoft's focus on productivity software, its success with Windows and Xbox, and its challenges with mobile and cloud computing.

Section 3: Apple In this section, we'll take a closer look at Apple, its history, and its unique position in the tech industry. We'll explore Apple's strengths in hardware and design, its success with the iPhone and other mobile devices, and its challenges with software and innovation.

Section 4: Competition and Collaboration In this section, we'll explore how these tech giants compete with each other and collaborate on key projects. We'll discuss how Google, Microsoft, and Apple have challenged each other in the areas of search, mobile devices, and productivity software. We'll also explore how they have collaborated on projects like cross-platform compatibility and cloud computing.

Section 5: What's Next? In this section, we'll explore what the future holds for these tech giants and the tech industry as a whole. We'll discuss emerging technologies like AI, blockchain, and quantum computing, and how they could shape the industry in the years to come. We'll also discuss how Google, Microsoft, and Apple are positioning themselves for the future, and how they plan to stay ahead of the competition.

Conclusion: The competition between Google, Microsoft, and Apple is fierce, with each company constantly pushing the limits of innovation and bringing new products and services to market. While each company has its own unique strengths and weaknesses, they all share a commitment to delivering value to their customers and driving the tech industry forward. As we look to the future, it will be exciting to see how these tech giants continue to innovate and shape the world we live in.

Google's controversial actions, such as its relationship with China and privacy concerns.

Google is one of the world's largest technology companies, known for its search engine, cloud computing, and other products and services. However, the company has also been the subject of controversy in recent years due to its actions and decisions on a range of issues, from data privacy to censorship and relationships with authoritarian regimes. In this article, we will explore some of the controversial actions and decisions that Google has made, and the implications for the company, its users, and the wider tech industry.

Google in China

One of the most controversial actions taken by Google in recent years has been its relationship with the Chinese government. In 2010, the company decided to stop censoring its search results in China, and as a result, its search engine was blocked in the country. However, in recent years, there have been reports that Google is considering re-entering the Chinese market, with a censored search engine that would comply with the country's strict censorship laws.

The move has been met with criticism from human rights groups and activists, who argue that Google's cooperation with the Chinese government would be a betrayal of its values and principles. Critics have also pointed out that Google's decision to comply with Chinese censorship laws could set a dangerous precedent for other tech companies, and give authoritarian regimes more power to control the flow of information.

Privacy Concerns

Google has also been the subject of numerous privacy concerns over the years, with critics arguing that the company collects and uses too much data on its users. In 2012, the company was fined $22.5 million by the Federal Trade Commission (FTC) for tracking users of Apple's Safari browser without their consent. The company has also been accused of tracking the location of Android users even when they have turned off location services.

In addition to these concerns, Google has also been criticized for its use of data for targeted advertising. The company collects a vast amount of information on its users, including search history, location data, and other browsing information. This information is then used to serve targeted ads, which has raised concerns about the company's privacy practices and the potential for data breaches.

Antitrust Investigations

In recent years, Google has also faced a number of antitrust investigations from regulators around the world. In 2017, the European Union fined Google $2.7 billion for antitrust violations related to its shopping search service. The company has also been accused of using its dominance in the search engine market to suppress competition in other areas, such as online advertising and mobile devices.

Google's critics argue that the company's market dominance gives it too much power to control the flow of information and stifle innovation. In response to these concerns, some have called for the company to be broken up or regulated more heavily.

Conclusion

Google is a complex and influential company that has made significant contributions to the world of technology. However, its actions and decisions in recent years have also been the subject of controversy and criticism. From its relationship with the Chinese government to its privacy practices and antitrust issues, Google faces a range of challenges and concerns that will shape its future and the future of the tech industry as a whole.

Moving forward, it will be important for Google to balance its desire to innovate and grow with its responsibility to its users and the wider society. The company will need to continue to engage with stakeholders and regulators to address these issues and find solutions that promote innovation and competition while also protecting user privacy and data. Ultimately, the success of Google and the tech industry as a whole will depend on how well it can navigate these complex and evolving challenges.

Continuing from the previous article, here are some more controversial actions and decisions taken by Google.

Content Moderation

Google has faced criticism for its content moderation policies on various platforms, including YouTube and

Google Play. In particular, the company has been accused of not doing enough to prevent the spread of hate speech, harassment, and misinformation. In 2017, major brands began to boycott YouTube after their ads were found to be running alongside extremist content. In response, Google introduced stricter content moderation policies and increased the number of moderators reviewing content.

However, Google's efforts to combat misinformation and hate speech have also been met with criticism from some quarters. Critics argue that the company's policies are too broad and can lead to censorship of legitimate speech. Some have also accused the company of applying its policies inconsistently and not doing enough to protect the free expression of marginalized communities.

Worker Activism

Google has also faced internal criticism from its own employees, who have spoken out against the company's controversial decisions and policies. In 2018, thousands of employees protested the company's involvement in a Pentagon program that used Google's artificial intelligence technology for drone warfare. Later that year, employees organized a walkout to protest the company's handling of sexual harassment claims.

Worker activism has become a growing concern for tech companies, who are facing increased scrutiny and pressure from their employees to do more to promote ethical and socially responsible practices. Google's handling of these protests has been criticized by some who argue that the company has not done enough to listen to the concerns of its employees or to address their grievances.

Conclusion

Google's controversial actions and decisions have raised important questions about the role of tech companies in society and the responsibility they have to their users and stakeholders. As the company continues to grow and evolve, it will be important for it to navigate these complex issues and find ways to balance innovation with social responsibility.

The tech industry as a whole is facing increasing scrutiny and regulation, and it is clear that companies like Google will need to take proactive steps to address these concerns and build trust with their users and stakeholders. Whether it is in the areas of privacy, content moderation, or worker activism, the success of tech companies will depend on their ability to engage with the wider society and find ways to promote innovation while also respecting the rights and values of their users.

Google's Impact on the Media Industry

Over the past two decades, Google has emerged as one of the most dominant forces in the media industry. With its powerful search engine and other tools, the company has transformed the way people access and consume news and information. However, Google's impact on the media industry has not been without controversy and criticism. In this article, we will explore the ways in which Google has impacted the media industry and examine the concerns and challenges that have arisen as a result.

The Rise of Search Engines

Before the advent of search engines, the media industry was largely dominated by traditional news outlets such as newspapers and television networks. However, with the rise of search engines, the way people access and consume news and information has changed dramatically. Google has emerged as the dominant player in the search engine space, with more than 90% of the global market share.

The rise of search engines has had both positive and negative impacts on the media industry. On the positive side, search engines have made it easier for people to access information from a wide range of sources. This has led to greater democratization of the media landscape, with a wider range of voices and perspectives represented in the online space.

However, there are also concerns about the impact of search engines on the media industry. Critics argue that search engines have disrupted the traditional business model of news outlets by siphoning off their advertising revenue. Because search engines generate their revenue through advertising, they have been able to offer access to news content for free, making it more difficult for traditional news outlets to compete.

The Rise of Google News

In addition to its search engine, Google also offers a news aggregation service called Google News. This service automatically aggregates news articles from a wide range of sources and presents them in a single feed. While Google News has become a popular tool for many users, it has also raised concerns about the impact of aggregation on the media industry.

One of the main criticisms of Google News is that it devalues the original reporting and journalism that goes into creating news content. Because Google News aggregates content from a wide range of sources, it can be difficult for individual news outlets to distinguish their content from that of their competitors. This has led to concerns that the aggregation of news content could lead to a reduction in the quality and diversity of news reporting.

The Impact on Advertising

One of the ways in which Google has disrupted the media industry is through its impact on advertising. With its powerful advertising platform, Google has become one of the dominant players in the online advertising space. This has led to concerns about the impact of advertising on the media industry, particularly in relation to the issue of fake news.

Fake news has become a major concern in recent years, with many people using social media and other online platforms to spread false information. Google has been accused of not doing enough to combat the spread of fake news, and some critics have argued that its advertising platform has actually helped to promote it. By allowing advertisers to target users based on their search history and other data, Google has created a system that can be easily exploited by those seeking to spread false information.

The Future of the Media Industry

As the media industry continues to evolve, it is clear that Google will play an increasingly important role in shaping its future. While the company has brought many benefits to the media industry, it has also raised important questions about the role of technology and the impact of new media on traditional news outlets.

Moving forward, it will be important for Google and other tech companies to work closely with the media industry to find ways to promote innovation and growth while also protecting the values and principles that underpin quality journalism. This will require a commitment to transparency, collaboration, and a shared vision for the future of the media

The challenges facing the company, such as increasing regulatory scrutiny and competition from other companies

In recent years, Google has faced a number of challenges that threaten its dominant position in the tech industry. These challenges range from increasing regulatory scrutiny to competition from other companies. In this article, we will take a closer look at these challenges and how they may impact Google's future.

Regulatory Scrutiny

Google is no stranger to regulatory scrutiny. In recent years, the company has been the subject of investigations by the European Union, the United States, and other regulatory bodies. These investigations have focused on a variety of issues, including Google's dominance in the search and advertising markets, its collection of user data, and its practices related to antitrust and competition.

The increased regulatory scrutiny of Google has the potential to significantly impact the company's business. For example, if regulators were to find that Google violated antitrust laws, they could force the company to change its business practices or break up its business into smaller companies. This would likely have a significant impact on Google's revenue and profitability.

Competition from Other Companies

Google has long been the dominant player in the search and advertising markets. However, in recent years, the company has faced increased competition from other tech giants, such as Amazon and Facebook. These companies are also investing heavily in search and advertising, and they are beginning to eat into Google's market share.

In addition to competition from other tech giants, Google is also facing competition from smaller, more nimble startups. These companies are able to quickly develop and launch new products and services, which can make it difficult for Google to keep up.

The increased competition from other companies is a major challenge for Google. The company will need to continue to innovate and develop new products and services in order to stay ahead of the competition.

In addition to regulatory scrutiny and competition, Google is also facing challenges related to privacy concerns and data security. As a company that collects and stores vast amounts of user data, Google has come under fire for its data collection practices and the potential for this data to be misused.

Google has taken steps to address these concerns, such as implementing stronger privacy controls and data protection measures. However, as more users become aware of the potential risks associated with sharing their data, Google will need to continue to prioritize data security and privacy to maintain their users' trust.

Another challenge facing Google is the changing nature of the tech industry itself. With the rise of artificial intelligence, virtual and augmented reality, and the Internet of Things, the tech landscape is constantly evolving. Google will need to keep up with these changes and adapt its business model and product offerings to remain relevant and competitive.

Finally, Google's size and reach have also made it a target for criticism on a variety of social and political issues, such as censorship and the spread of misinformation. As a company that plays a significant role in shaping the flow of information online, Google will need to address these concerns and work to ensure that its platform is used in a responsible and ethical manner.

Conclusion

Google is facing a number of challenges that have the potential to significantly impact its business. The increased regulatory scrutiny and competition from other companies are just two of the challenges that Google is currently facing. However, the company has a strong track record of innovation and adaptation, and it is likely that it will be able to overcome these challenges in the years ahead. As one of the world's largest and most successful tech companies, Google has the resources and talent necessary to navigate the changing landscape of the tech industry.

CHAPTER TWENTY-NINE

The potential impact of Google's future growth on society and the internet

Google is one of the most successful tech companies in the world. With a market capitalization of over $1 trillion and a global reach that touches the lives of billions of people, Google is a company with tremendous influence on society and the internet. However, as the company continues to grow and expand, there are concerns about the potential impact of its future growth on society and the internet. In this article, we will explore the potential impact of Google's future growth on society and the internet.

The Impact of Google's Search and Advertising Dominance

One of the most significant ways that Google has impacted society and the internet is through its dominance in the search and advertising markets. Google's search engine is the most popular in the world, with over 90% market share, and its advertising business is similarly dominant, accounting for over 30% of all digital advertising revenue worldwide.

While Google's dominance in these markets has led to tremendous success for the company, it has also raised concerns about the potential for anti-competitive behavior and the impact on the internet as a whole. For example, some critics argue that Google's control of the search market gives it an unfair advantage over competitors, and that the company may be using its dominant position to prioritize its own products and services over those of its competitors.

Furthermore, as Google's advertising business continues to grow, there are concerns about the impact on the internet as a whole. Some critics argue that the proliferation of online advertising has led to a decline in the quality of content online, as websites and publishers are incentivized to produce clickbait and other low-quality content in order to generate ad revenue.

The Impact of Google's Data Collection and Use

Another significant way that Google has impacted society and the internet is through its collection and use of user data. Google collects vast amounts of data on its users, including search history, location data, and personal preferences. This data is then used to personalize the user experience and to target advertising.

While personalized experiences and targeted advertising can be beneficial for users and advertisers alike, there are concerns about the potential for this data to be misused. For example, there have been instances of data breaches and data misuse at other tech companies, and some critics worry that Google's vast trove of user data could be a target for hackers or could be used for nefarious purposes.

Furthermore, as Google continues to expand its business into new areas such as healthcare and finance, there are concerns about the potential for the company to further collect and use sensitive user data. While there are potential benefits to these new areas of business, such as improved healthcare outcomes or personalized financial services, there are also concerns about the privacy and security implications of these activities.

The Impact of Google's Role in the Spread of Information

As one of the largest and most popular platforms for accessing information online, Google has a significant role to play in the spread of information and the shaping of public discourse. Google's algorithms and search results can have a significant impact on what information is seen and shared online, and the company has been criticized for its role in spreading misinformation and fake news.

While Google has taken steps to address this issue, such as implementing fact-checking tools and updating its algorithms to prioritize high-quality content, there are concerns about the potential for the company to further shape public discourse and opinion. For example, as Google expands its role in areas such as artificial intelligence and machine learning, there are concerns about the potential for these technologies to be used to further manipulate and shape public opinion.

CHAPTER THIRTY

Google Resume

Google is one of the most desirable employers in the world, and as such, the company receives thousands of applications every day. To help manage this volume, Google uses a variety of tools and techniques to identify the best candidates for each position. One of the most important of these tools is the candidate's Curriculum Vitae, or CV.

The role of a CV in Google's hiring process is to provide the company with a summary of the candidate's education, work experience, skills, and achievements. This information helps Google's recruiters and hiring managers assess whether the candidate has the necessary qualifications for the position and whether they are a good fit for the company's culture.

When reviewing a CV, Google's recruiters and hiring managers look for a number of key factors. These include:

Relevant education and work experience: Google typically requires candidates to have a college degree in a relevant field and relevant work experience. The candidate's CV should clearly show that they have the necessary education and experience for the position.

Specific skills and achievements: Google looks for candidates with specific skills and achievements that are relevant to the position. For example, if the position requires programming skills, the candidate's CV should show that they have experience with programming languages such as Python, Java, or C++. Similarly, if the position requires experience with project management, the candidate's CV should show that they have successfully managed projects in the past.

Impact and results: Google values candidates who have made a significant impact in their previous roles. The candidate's CV should highlight specific achievements, such as increasing revenue, improving efficiency, or launching a successful product.

Diversity and inclusion: Google is committed to building a diverse and inclusive workforce, and the company looks for candidates who share this commitment. The candidate's CV should demonstrate that they have experience working with diverse teams and that they value diversity and inclusion.

In addition to these factors, Google's recruiters and hiring managers also look for qualities such as passion, creativity, and problem-solving ability. The candidate's CV should give some indication of these qualities, either through their work experience or through extracurricular activities or hobbies.

It is important to note that while a strong CV is an important part of the hiring process at Google, it is not the only factor that the company considers. Google also uses a variety of other tools and techniques, such as interviews, coding challenges, and reference checks, to assess a candidate's skills and fit for the position. However, a well-crafted CV can be an important first step in the process of landing a job at Google.